Guess Who
Swims

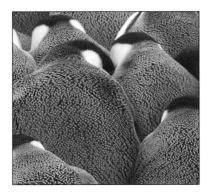

Dana Meachen Rau

Marshall Cavendish
Benchmark
New York

I swim in the sea.

I can dive very deep.

I eat fish.

I grab them with my *beak*.

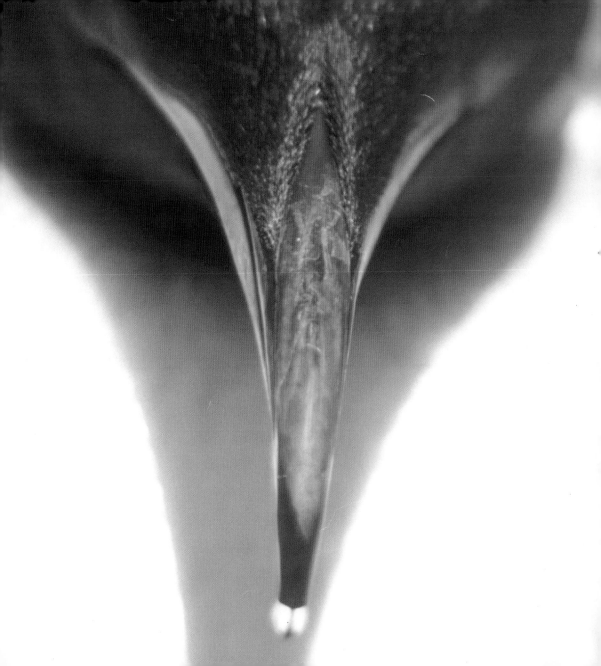

I have black and white feathers.

My feathers keep me dry.

I have wings.

But I do not fly.

My wings help me swim.

I can swim for a long time.

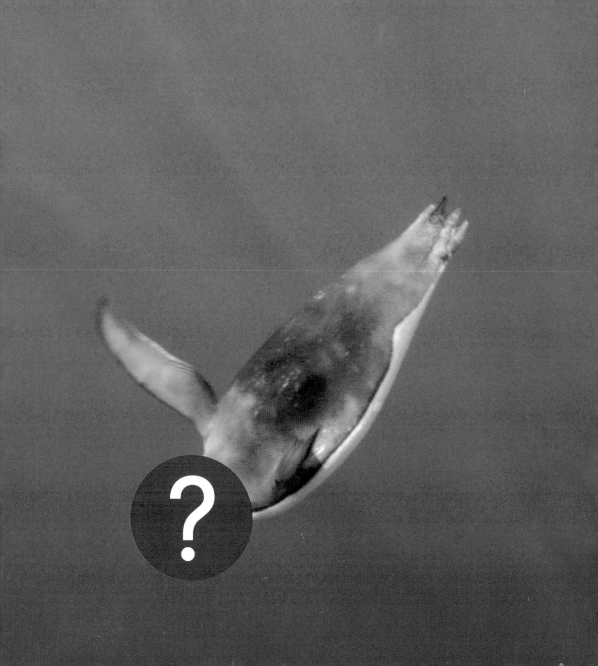

My feet help me swim.

My feet help me walk, too.

I live on the ice.

The ice is cold.

I live in a group.

My group is called a *colony*.

My colony is noisy.

We call to each other.

I lay one egg.

It has to stay warm.

My baby is a *chick*.

It has soft gray feathers.

I slide on my belly.

Who am I?

I am a penguin!

Who am I?

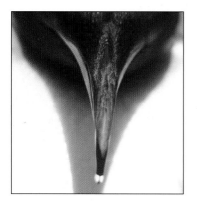
beak

chick

colony

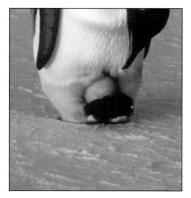
egg

feathers

feet   **ice**   **wings**

Challenge Words

beak (beek) The sharp, hard, pointy mouth part of a bird.

chick (chik) A baby penguin.

colony (KAHL-uh-nee) A group of penguins that live together.

Index

Page numbers in **boldface** are illustrations.

About the Author

Dana Meachen Rau is the author of many other titles in the Bookworms series, as well as other nonfiction and early reader books. She lives in Burlington, Connecticut, with her husband and two children.

With thanks to the Reading Consultants:

Nanci Vargus, Ed.D., is an Assistant Professor of Elementary Education at the University of Indianapolis.

Beth Walker Gambro is an Adjunct Professor at the University of St. Francis in Joliet, Illinois.

Marshall Cavendish Benchmark
99 White Plains Road
Tarrytown, New York 10591-5502
www.marshallcavendish.us

Library of Congress Cataloging-in-Publication Data

Rau, Dana Meachen, 1971–
Guess who swims / by Dana Meachen Rau.
p. cm. — (Bookworms. Guess who)
Summary: "Following a guessing game format, this book provides young readers with
clues about a penguin's physical characteristics, behaviors, and habitats, challenging readers
to identify it"—Provided by publisher.
Includes index.
ISBN 978-0-7614-2974-6
1. Penguins—Juvenile literature. I. Title. II. Series.
QL696.S473R38 2009
598.47—dc22
2007024611

Editor: Christina Gardeski
Publisher: Michelle Bisson
Designer: Virginia Pope
Art Director: Anahid Hamparian

Photo Research by Anne Burns Images

Cover Photo by *Animals Animals*/Gerald L. Kooyman

The photographs in this book are used with permission and through the courtesy of:
Peter Arnold: pp. 1, 17, 28TR BIOS Andre Loic; pp. 7, 15, 28BR, 29C Fritz Polking;
pp. 9, 27, 29R S. Muller. *Animals Animals*: pp. 3, 5, 28TL Gerald L. Kooyman;
pp. 11, 21, 28BL Doug Allan/OSF; pp. 13, 29L Johnny Johnson; p. 25 Ben Osborne/OSF.
SuperStock: p. 19 age fotostock. *Corbis*: pp. 23, 28TC Frans Lanting.

Printed in Malaysia
1   3   5   6   4   2